HOW TO WORRY LESS

TIPS AND TECHNIQUES TO HELP YOU FIND CALM

CLAIRE CHAMBERLAIN

HOW TO WORRY LESS

An Hachette UK Company
www.hachette.co.uk

Vie Books, an imprint of Summersdale Publishers Ltd
Part of Octopus Publishing Group Limited
Carmelite House
50 Victoria Embankment
LONDON
EC4Y 0DZ
UK

www.summersdale.com

Printed and bound in China

ISBN: 978-1-80007-171-1

Substantial discounts on bulk quantities of Summersdale books are available to corporations, professional associations and other organizations. For details contact general enquiries: telephone: +44 (0) 1243 771107 or email: enquiries@summersdale.com.

CONTENTS

INTRODUCTION

There's a famous saying: "Worry is like a rocking chair. It gives you something to do, but doesn't get you anywhere." How often have worries darted around in your head, leaving you with feelings of stress and anxiety, but with no solutions?

We all experience worry from time to time. Sometimes it can be helpful, spurring you on to take action where necessary. But it can also start to take a toll on your mental health, disrupting your peace of mind. If your worries become too severe, it's a good idea to seek professional help. But by taking some simple steps, it's possible to get those worries under control and start enjoying life again!

This book is filled with useful information, practical tips and inspiring ideas, all of which can help you on the road toward a worry-free life. Are you ready to dive in?

CHAPTER ONE

UNDERSTANDING WORRY

We've probably all faced situations or events that we've worried about. But what *is* worry? It can sometimes feel hard to define. Broadly speaking, when you worry your mind engages in repetitive thoughts, images, ideas or feelings, often linked to uncertainty or fear, in relation to the future. The uncertainty aspect is key here: the future is always unknown and so our mind tends to flit between several (or many) potential negative outcomes, playing them over on a loop. Worries can fall into several categories: big or small; everyday or chronic; solvable or unsolvable; reasonable or abstract. We'll explore these ideas further throughout this chapter.

WORRY PRETENDS TO BE
NECESSARY BUT SERVES
NO USEFUL PURPOSE.

ECKHART TOLLE

WHY WORRY?

Just as we are all unique individuals, we will all have unique fears and worries. Two people could be faced with the same future scenario and yet they will both have a different response to it. When we find ourselves worrying about something that a friend isn't giving a second thought to, it does not make us weak. Whether we worry about something or not often comes down to (among other things) our past experiences, how resilient we are feeling in that particular moment, how well we perceive other areas of our life are going and how supported we feel. The amount we worry is never set in stone. There are ways we can learn to rationalize our fears, as well as building and strengthening our mental resilience.

WORRY vs ANXIETY

The words "worry" and "anxiety" are often used interchangeably, but there are some key psychological (and physiological) differences. Worrying tends to be purely thought-based, in relation to a specific event or problem. Anxiety, on the other hand, relates to your body's physiological response to fear: the "fight, flight or freeze" response. It can be harder to identify the cause of anxiety, as it is less specific and often more overwhelming. Because worrying thoughts can trigger anxiety, it's important to learn how to control worry, to stop it getting out of hand.

WORRY IS INTEREST PAID
ON TROUBLE BEFORE IT
COMES DUE.

WILLIAM RALPH INGE

WHY WORRY?

While it can be annoying, distressing and upsetting, worry has had an important function in our evolution as a species. Without it, it's unlikely we would be here today. The worries of our ancestors – including where food was going to come from and how to protect against predators – would have instigated crucial problem-solving and lateral thinking, which continues to this day: worrying about solvable problems pushes us to search for solutions. In fact, worries only become a problem when they spiral out of control.

YOU ARE STRONGER THAN ALL OF THE OBSTACLES STANDING IN YOUR WAY

COMMON
WORRIES

If you worry often – especially if your worries keep you awake at night or if you find you worry constantly – you might feel very alone with your fears, as if you're the only person battling worry. But you're really not. Pretty much everyone knows what it feels like to worry and most people's worries will be significant at some point in their lives. As with everything in life, worries will fluctuate. Sometimes you'll go through periods where life feels great, other times niggling worries will persistently enter your thoughts, disturbing your peace of mind. And while everyone's worries will be slightly different, there are often common themes: financial, employment, relationship and health worries are all common in adults. And remember, children worry, too. Just because a child's fears don't seem big to you, it doesn't mean they aren't big to them, so it's important to acknowledge everyone's worries, whatever their age.

YOU ARE BEAUTIFUL, GIFTED AND INTELLIGENT.

DON'T LET THE STORM MAKE YOU FORGET IT.

Russell T. Davies

FINANCIAL WORRIES

Unpaid bills, overdrafts and maxed-out credit cards can preoccupy your thoughts, as can unemployment or having to manage an irregular income. These problems often feel overwhelming, but remember there are always small steps you can take to start regaining control. Starting to pay off just one debt, obtaining advice from a financial support charity or drawing up a weekly budget (and sticking to it) are good first steps.

"YOU'RE ONLY HERE FOR
A SHORT VISIT. DON'T
HURRY, DON'T WORRY.
AND BE SURE TO SMELL THE
FLOWERS ALONG THE WAY.

WALTER HAGEN

RELATIONSHIP WORRIES

From conflict issues to fears of abandonment, relationship worries can have a big impact on your life. How you move forward will very much depend on the cause. If you struggle with trust, for example, is this due to a previous betrayal, or is your current partner's behaviour the problem? Take time to decide the best way forward. With love and acceptance, you and your partner might be able to navigate these problems. But listen to your instinct: if something isn't right, it's OK to question whether it's time to walk away.

WHAT MAKES YOU HAPPY? MAKE TIME FOR IT TODAY

HEALTH WORRIES

Often, a diagnosis of a health condition or illness (whether physical or mental) can bring with it stress, worry and anxiety. You may have fears for your own (or your family's) future and if you're suddenly unable to work that can bring financial strain, too. Health conditions often bring with them huge amounts of uncertainty. If you're worried about an illness or condition, however minor you think it may be, don't put off a visit to your doctor — taking control by addressing the issue is always the best course of action. Remember, you don't need to suffer in silence: if you're struggling to come to terms with a diagnosis, trained counsellors can offer help, support and advice.

IS WORRY EVER HELPFUL?

While worrying doesn't feel particularly nice, it can serve a valuable purpose, as long as your worries are reasonable and solvable. For example, if you have an exam coming up, worrying about whether you are going to pass will lead to action, in this case revision, so you are as prepared as you can be. This worry is reasonable (you don't want to fail) and solvable (you can create a study plan in the weeks leading up to the test). If you find yourself worrying, it's always a good idea to dissect those niggling concerns in the back your mind, to see if you can proactively address your worries.

WORRYING DOESN'T
STOP THE BAD STUFF
FROM HAPPENING.
IT JUST STOPS YOU
FROM ENJOYING
THE GOOD STUFF.

KAREN SALMANSOHN

CHANGE YOUR LANGUAGE

It can be worth considering changing your language around worry, to help break its repetitive cycle in your mind. Constantly running your worries over and over in your head is not going to get you very far. Try breaking the cycle with a "but..." to help you move forward with a more positive mindset. For example, "I'm worried, **but** I know I am going to get through this" or "I'm worried, **but** I know it's unlikely my fears will materialize." Reframing worry in this way can be highly effective, as it breaks the unhelpful loop.

IF IT DOESN'T BRING YOU JOY, DO YOU REALLY NEED IT IN YOUR LIFE?

CHRONIC WORRYING

Concerns, worries and doubts are all a normal part of life: they come and go like grey clouds across a blue sky. Often they can be resolved fairly swiftly or, if not resolved, then their prominence in your life diminishes. But what if your worrying has become chronic? If your "everyday" worries seem to be out of control, and you feel constantly up against uncontrollable worries, negative thoughts and worst case "what if" scenarios, you may have chronic worry. Chronic worrying can disrupt your emotional balance, play havoc with your mental and emotional health, and start to interfere with your daily life. It's also a symptom of generalized anxiety disorder (GAD), as well as other anxiety disorders. Chronic worrying can seem an unsolvable problem in itself, but there are steps you can take to ease its grip on your life.

BREATHE IN DEEPLY

EXHALE SLOWLY

SYMPTOMS OF WORRY

Excessive worrying is a common symptom of an anxiety disorder, but it can also create symptoms of its own. As well as mental and emotional symptoms – such as a racing mind and repetitive, negative thought patterns – physical symptoms of worry can include headaches, "butterflies" in your stomach, nausea and loss of appetite. These physical symptoms are more commonly associated with anxiety, so if you are suffering it can be a good idea to speak with a medical professional for support and advice.

"

YOU MAY NOT CONTROL
ALL THE EVENTS THAT
HAPPEN TO YOU, BUT YOU
CAN DECIDE NOT TO BE
REDUCED BY THEM.

MAYA ANGELOU

YOU ARE PERFECT EXACTLY AS YOU ARE

IMAGINE HOW WE
WOULD BE IF WE WERE
LESS AFRAID.

CHARLIE MACKESY

SLEEPLESS NIGHTS

If you suffer with chronic worry, you may find it hard to sleep at night. Sleep problems – such as difficulty drifting off, frequent night waking or waking too early – can go hand in hand with worry, as your mind struggles to switch off. Making time to relax in the hour before you head to bed can help. Avoid screens and instead take a bath, unwind with a book or try meditation.

SPEAK KINDLY TO YOURSELF, TODAY AND ALWAYS

GETTING TO GRIPS WITH WORRY

Acknowledging that your worries might be spiralling out of control is an important first step when it comes to starting to manage (and move beyond) them. Feeling like something is wrong can be upsetting and uncomfortable, but you are not the only person who is in this place right now – not by a long shot! The moment that you accept there may be a problem is also a moment of so many possibilities. Tackling your demons and challenging ingrained thought patterns can be hard, but by putting in the work and taking a deep dive into your thoughts, feelings and emotions, you could find yourself in a much happier, more content place. In the midst of negative thought spirals, it can seem there is no way out. But there is. Always.

I JUST THINK YOU CAN'T
LET YOUR DEMONS RUIN
YOUR DAY.

BRYONY GORDON

KEEP TRACK OF YOUR WORRIES

When getting to grips with worry, it can be a good idea to keep a mood diary. Each day, jot down how you've been feeling, alongside other key factors, including what you've eaten (and when), how well you've slept, how much fresh air and exercise you've had and (if you have periods) where you are in your menstrual cycle. Try to keep your notes for at least six weeks and then look back. Have any patterns emerged? Perhaps you can spot particular triggers for your worry spirals.

THIS MOMENT IS A FRESH START. SEIZE IT.

YOUR ACTION PLAN

/////////////////////////////////////

By now you might have a better idea of why you worry and what your particular triggers are, but this alone is not enough to help you. To instigate meaningful change, you'll need a positive action plan that will help you build resilience, boost your mindset, and supercharge both your mental and physical health. Let's go!

YOU MIGHT NOT KNOW WHAT COMES NEXT, BUT THAT'S OK

CHAPTER TWO

CALM
THE MIND

If you suffer with chronic worry, you probably spend a lot of time lost inside your own head, getting caught up in a cycle of negative thought spirals. Because the fact of the matter is, while you might often *feel* worry in your body – as fluttering nerves or a dry mouth, for example – all worry happens in the mind. But if you can calm your mind, change your thoughts and begin to feel more connected to your body, those worries and negative thoughts will likely ease. This chapter is full of tips and techniques to help you move beyond your worries and rationalize your fears.

WHAT IS MINDFULNESS?

Becoming more mindful in everyday life is a wonderful antidote to worry. Mindfulness is simply the act of becoming consciously aware of the present moment, exactly as it is and without judgement. Reconnecting with the present moment like this, without willing anything to be different, is a way of temporarily silencing any worries or anxieties you may be ruminating on – worries that, more often than not, stop you from experiencing the present moment fully. Your mind cannot be completely focused on the here and now while also worrying about the future. Think about it for a minute: if you are truly engaged with the sound of the breeze rustling the leaves on the trees in your garden, and the colour of them, and the smell of the earth, it's hard to continue worrying about something else.

LIVE
MORE
MINDFULLY

Mindfulness sounds simple – and it is – but often you are so used to being caught up inside your mind, it can take a while to get the hang of it. Start when your mind feels relatively at ease, then slowly draw your attention to your present surroundings. Focus in turn on what you can see, hear, smell, touch and even taste. How does your body feel right now – tense or relaxed? Mindfulness is not about judgement: it is simply about conscious awareness. You don't need to change anything, simply notice. In time, living more mindfully can help you feel more at ease in each moment.

"

I DON'T HAVE TO CHASE
EXTRAORDINARY MOMENTS
TO FIND HAPPINESS – IT'S
RIGHT IN FRONT OF ME IF
I'M PAYING ATTENTION
AND PRACTISING
GRATITUDE.

BRENÉ BROWN

CHOOSE A MANTRA

A mantra is a word, phrase or even sound that is repeated over and over again. Traditionally used during meditation or yoga, mantra is a Sanskrit word that literally translates as "instrument of thought" and, as such, it can be used to focus your mind on a positive intention. Choose a mantra that truly resonates with you and repeat it each morning to help calm your brain and strengthen your mindset. Examples include: "I embrace each moment" or "I accept what is".

STEP INTO TODAY WITH COURAGE. YOU'VE GOT THIS!

LET THOUGHTS PASS

Many of us buy into our thoughts to such an extent that they start to become our reality. In fact, it's easy to forget the truth: that thoughts are just thoughts. Unfortunately, if you start to really believe some of the negative thoughts you have, it can cause you a lot of unnecessary pain, sadness and stress. For example, have you ever found yourself thinking: *I'm not pretty/clever/interesting/funny enough*? It can seem true, can't it? But it's not. From now on, instead of listening to and believing every thought you have about yourself and the world around you, aim to simply then let them pass by, without attachment. You may like to challenge your negative thoughts, especially if they are particularly damaging, but make sure you don't engage with them for too long. For example, if you find yourself unconsciously thinking, "I'm just not pretty," counter this thought with, "I am a beautiful human, inside and out," and then move on. Spending too much time arguing inside your head can stop you fully living your brilliant and precious life.

THE HAPPINESS IN YOUR LIFE DEPENDS ON

THE QUALITY OF YOUR THOUGHTS.

Katie Piper

EMBRACE UNCERTAINTY

Not knowing what's around the corner can leave you feeling vulnerable. But the truth is, more often than not, you really *don't* know what's around the corner: no matter how much planning, organizing and preparation you do, no one really knows what's in store. If you resist this uncertainty, it will only cause worry, fear and unrest. Instead, learn to accept and embrace the uncertainty of life: try to view it as exciting rather than worrying. It's OK to not know exactly what lies ahead.

MAYBE THE POINT OF LIFE IS TO GIVE UP CERTAINTY AND TO EMBRACE LIFE'S BEAUTIFUL UNCERTAINTY.

MATT HAIG

THINK POSITIVE

Does your mind tend to offer up a host of potential bad outcomes each time you contemplate doing something new or different? You know the ones: "What if I fail?" "What if they don't like me?" "What if I'm not good enough?" You don't have to listen. Remember, it's in your power to override these with positive "what ifs". And it's always worth ignoring your worries and doing it anyway. Because what if you succeed? What if they love you? What if you're brilliant?

WHAT IF... IT ALL WORKS OUT PERFECTLY?

TRY
MEDITATION

Meditation can be a powerful tool to help move your awareness away from your thoughts. While similar to mindfulness, meditation is a practice that will see you focus your attention on to a single thing (such as your breath) for an extended period, whereas mindfulness sees you focus on the present moment and everything in it (including sights, smells and sounds). In a way, meditation is about blocking out all external noise, while mindfulness is about embracing it. Research shows that a regular meditation practice can reduce stress, lessen anxiety and enhance self-awareness. There are many different ways to meditate, some of which we will cover over the next few pages, but generally it's common practice to draw your attention to your breath, different areas of your body or an external object, such as a candle flame or crystal. As you meditate, you may find your mind wanders as thoughts arise in your head. This is perfectly normal: as soon as you notice these thoughts, simply acknowledge them, then draw your attention back to the object of your attention, for example, your breath. If you're unsure how to get started, guided meditations are a great entry point – you can find them online or via a meditation app.

THE BODY SCAN

This meditation is a wonderful way to draw your attention out of your mind and into your body, helping you to feel grounded and more self-aware. To begin, sit or lie comfortably and close your eyes, focusing on each inhale and exhale for a few breaths. Then slowly draw your attention to your feet: feel the weight of them on the floor. Are they comfortable or uncomfortable? Notice, without judging or trying to change anything. Then slowly move your attention up your body, focusing on each area in turn. This meditation can lead to a deep sense of relaxation and ease.

YOU ARE THE SKY.
EVERYTHING ELSE – IT'S
JUST THE WEATHER.

PEMA CHÖDRÖN

FOLLOW YOUR BREATH

We take roughly 25,000 breaths each and every day, but how often do you think about doing it? This meditation brings your awareness to your breath, to help still your mind. Close your eyes and focus your attention on the rise of your stomach and chest as you breathe in, then notice them fall as you slowly exhale. If your mind wanders, you might like to count your breaths: one to inhale, two to exhale, and so on up to ten, then start again. Even just a few minutes can make a difference to the way you feel.

SLOW DOWN AND FIND PEACE IN THE STILLNESS

TAKE POSITIVE ACTION

Often, pushing your concerns aside and ignoring them can lead to further anxiety, as those troublesome thoughts and worries play in the back of your mind. Instead, try to listen to your worries when they first present themselves. Is there any positive action you can take to solve the matter? Even fears that at first seem too large to manage, such as financial worries, can be handled if you take small steps, such as making an appointment to speak with your bank.

If you have worries that seem so vast they appear unsolvable or require collective action, are there small actions that you *can* take? For example, perhaps you feel increasingly anxious about climate change. What changes could you make in your own life that would help to reduce carbon emissions? Could you switch to a green energy provider or green bank, reduce your meat intake or commit to avoiding single-use plastic? Which petitions could you sign? Taking proactive steps, however small, can help you to feel more empowered and in control.

BE PROACTIVE

YOU CAN MAKE A DIFFERENCE

GROUND YOURSELF

Getting lost in negative thought spirals can leave you feeling jittery and unsettled. If your inner voice is amplifying your fears and worries, it can even lead to sensations of disassociation or panic attacks. If you start to feel panic take hold, attempt to physically ground yourself: start to pay attention to the feel of your physical body in its surroundings. Notice the cool air on your skin, or the feel of your clothes, or the sensation of your body pressed into a chair, or your feet on the floor. Being physically present can help to diminish your sense of fear.

"

YOU CAN'T
STOP THE WAVES,
BUT YOU CAN
LEARN TO SURF.

JON KABAT-ZINN

CREATE WORRY TIME

Designating a 20-minute window each evening for "worry time" can help to stop you worrying on and off throughout each day. Every time a worrying thought pops into your head, stop it in its tracks and tell yourself you will deal with it later, at your specified time. Then carry on with your day. Chances are, by the time you reach the evening, you won't even remember what it was you were worried about or the issue will have already resolved itself.

DIFFICULT
TIMES ARISE
FOR EVERYONE,
BUT THEY DO
PASS – HANG
IN THERE

TRAIN YOUR BRAIN

Using pessimistic language can be highly damaging. Ask yourself: "How catastrophic is my inner voice?" Constantly telling yourself, "I'm so useless", "I've just ruined everything", or "This is the worst thing that could have happened", is never going to lessen your worries. Instead, each time that negative voice pops into your head, challenge it. For example, next time you notice that you're automatically telling yourself you have ruined everything, remember that you are human and you made a simple mistake. It happens. Now, how can you rectify it and move on? Research shows that by repeatedly training your brain to think differently in response to negative events you can actually rewrite neural pathways, meaning that over time a more positive response will be second nature.

BEING POSITIVE DOESN'T
MEAN YOU DON'T EVER
HAVE NEGATIVE THOUGHTS.
IT JUST MEANS YOU DON'T
LET THOSE THOUGHTS
CONTROL YOUR LIFE.

JAY SHETTY

LIFE ISN'T PERFECT

It's important to remember that life is not perfect for anyone. Difficult and painful situations are going to arise for us all, such as loss, illness and bereavement. But worrying about these difficult times is only going to add an extra layer of suffering on top of the pain. Focusing on the good in each and every moment can help, and accepting, acknowledging and riding out difficult times rather than trying to shy away from them can help to ease the suffering.

THE ATTEMPT TO ESCAPE
FROM PAIN IS WHAT
CREATES MORE PAIN.

GABOR MATÉ

CHANGE YOUR FOCUS

Are you forever trying to come up with solutions for things that haven't even happened yet? While contingency plans can be helpful, spending too much time caught up in potential future scenarios can lead to anxiety, because we can't actually deal with future problems – the only time and place we can take positive action is right now. Focusing on what *is*, rather than worrying about what *might be*, is important for good mental health.

EVERY STEP YOU TAKE ADDS UP SO KEEP GOING!

CHAPTER THREE

THE WORRY TOOLKIT

As you get lost in a spiral of negative thoughts and anxiety, it's often easy to neglect yourself and your needs. But at times of worry, looking after your physical health and happiness is vital. When you prioritize your well-being, it can help to lift your mood and make those tricky times feel a lot more manageable. The following pages offer some ideas on how to look after yourself during times of stress – your own personal worry toolkit!

YOUR HAPPINESS MATTERS: IT'S TIME TO PRIORITIZE IT

"

IT'S NOT SELFISH TO LOVE
YOURSELF, TAKE CARE OF
YOURSELF AND MAKE YOUR
HAPPINESS A PRIORITY.
IT'S NECESSARY.

MANDY HALE

WHAT IS SELF-CARE?

Self-care is the practice of consciously and actively taking steps to take care of yourself. The term encompasses looking after your physical, mental, emotional and spiritual well-being, and can involve things as small as regularly drinking water, taking a relaxing bath or curling up on the sofa with a good book for 20 minutes. And while the acts themselves can be very simple, the benefits can be huge: evidence suggests that instilling a regular self-care practice can do everything from improving your physical health and fitness, to reducing stress and anxiety, improving overall mental health and giving your self-esteem a boost. Self-care is very easy in theory, but think for a moment: how often do you consciously and deliberately look after your own well-being? Perhaps now is the time to start?

SELF-CARE BARRIERS

//

Two of the biggest barriers to self-care are lack of time and guilt. These days many of us have an ever-growing to-do list and with so much time pressure self-care is the first thing that gets pushed aside. What's more, our various responsibilities mean taking time out for ourselves often makes us feel guilty, especially if part of our role is caring for others. But remember, your health is important. It's time to start prioritizing yourself!

THE MORE THAT WE CAN
BRING OUR AUTHENTIC
SELVES, WITH HOPE, INTO
THE MOMENT – THE MORE
THAT MOMENT WILL SHOW
UP FOR US.

AMANDA GORMAN

CREATE HEALTHY HABITS

An easy step into self-care is to set one or two healthy daily habits that you feel will be simple to stick to. There are plenty of ways to improve your energy and health. Perhaps your goal could be to drink eight glasses of water daily, or to read a chapter of your book instead of scrolling on your phone in the evening. Maybe vowing to get out for a 10-minute brisk walk at lunchtime would be achievable, or perhaps you could aim to get to bed half an hour earlier each evening. Everyone is different, so our basic self-care needs will differ, too. Choose the ones that feel right for you.

ALWAYS BELIEVE IN YOURSELF – NO MATTER WHAT

MOVE MORE!

_____

Making time to move more, even if it's simply fitting in a short daily walk in the fresh air, has the capacity to free us somewhat from the stagnation of worry, stress and anxiety. In fact, exercise is well documented as being a fantastic stress-reliever, and has also been shown to help boost self-esteem, confidence, resilience and restore feelings of calm. If you're new to exercise, getting started can sometimes feel a bit intimidating or even overwhelming. One of the easiest ways to start is to simply vow to increase the number of steps you walk every day: walk instead of driving or hopping on the bus, take the stairs instead of the elevator and go for a walk at lunchtime instead of staying sedentary. Remember, it all adds up. You could even invest in a step counter for extra motivation.

THE STORM WILL PASS

HANG ON UNTIL IT DOES

EAT FOR POSITIVITY

What you eat and drink can have a big effect on the way you feel, both mentally and physically, so why not aim to be a little more conscious of what you're putting on your plate. Protein (such as fish, pulses, lean meat and eggs), complex carbohydrates (like brown rice and wholemeal bread), healthy fats (found in avocados and oily fish) and an array of colourful fruit and veg are all fantastic inclusions in your diet – and remember to drink six to eight glasses of water a day. Cooking from scratch is a great way to become more mindful of what you're eating, too.

I'VE BEEN SEARCHING FOR
WAYS TO HEAL MYSELF,
AND I'VE FOUND THAT
KINDNESS IS THE BEST WAY.

LADY GAGA

SLOWING
DOWN IS NOT
A SIGN OF
WEAKNESS;
IT'S A SIGN OF
SELF-LOVE

LOVING OTHER PEOPLE STARTS WITH LOVING OURSELVES AND ACCEPTING OURSELVES.

ELLIOT PAGE

START A JOURNAL

Most of us aren't in the habit of writing down our innermost thoughts and feelings regularly, so starting a journal might feel odd, or even uncomfortable, at first. But many people swear by journaling to help them make sense of their emotions, as well as helping them gain clarity and perspective. You don't need anything fancy to start – just a pen and notebook, and you're good to go! However, journaling has become something of an art form in recent years, so it's the perfect place to unleash your creative side and get doodling, drawing and colouring, as well as writing.

WHAT CAN YOU DO TODAY THAT WILL MAKE YOU SMILE?

TRY FOREST BATHING

It's well known that spending time in the natural world is far more relaxing than being surrounded by a concrete jungle. The sights, smells and sounds of nature, as well as the expanse of space and fresh air, are all wonderful tonics, helping to soothe frazzled souls. And those in the scientific and medical world concur: nature really is good for your soul. So much so, in fact, that some therapists now prescribe green exercise, and the Japanese tradition of *shinrin-yoku* (forest bathing) is being more widely adopted by Western cultures because of the proven benefits. These include reduced stress and anxiety, lowered blood pressure, boosted immunity and even alleviated depression. *Shinrin-yoku* simply involves spending time in a natural setting, such as a forest, woodland, meadow, park or seashore. There's nothing hurried about it and you're not exercising: it's simply about paying mindful attention to the environment that you are part of, as you sit or stroll slowly. A true tonic for the mind.

GET YOUR HANDS DIRTY

Growing and nurturing plants is wonderfully therapeutic and it's becoming ever more popular as a practical mindfulness tool. Even better is the fact that UK researchers have found that a type of friendly bacteria in soil activates brain cells to produce serotonin – a key hormone related to mood regulation and well-being. So, don't be afraid to get dirt under your fingernails! You don't need lots of space to see your plants thrive – a windowsill is the perfect place for herbs, tomatoes and chillis to grow.

WE HAVE SEASONS WHEN
WE FLOURISH AND SEASONS
WHEN THE LEAVES FALL
FROM US, REVEALING OUR
BARE BONES. GIVEN TIME,
THEY GROW AGAIN.

KATHERINE MAY

HAVE A LAUGH!

It might be the last thing you feel able to do in times of worry, but getting a fit of the giggles could be just what you need to help melt away worries. Studies show laughter can help to alleviate stress in numerous ways. For a start, a good belly laugh stimulates and then calms your stress response, heart rate and blood pressure, resulting in a feeling of peace. And that tension you're feeling? It might just melt away with a good chuckle, as laughing boosts circulation and promotes muscle relaxation. It could be time to pop on your favourite comedy box set.

DO WHAT MAKES YOUR SOUL SING

NURTURE YOUR CREATIVITY

Focusing your full attention on a creative project is a fabulous way to occupy your mind and help to reduce your stress and anxiety: by engaging with and immersing yourself in the task at hand you are distracted away from your worries. What's more, studies have shown that engaging in a creative activity for just 45 minutes can reduce the amount of cortisol (a stress hormone) in your body. Freeing your imagination and allowing yourself to create – whether that's by drawing, painting, writing, sculpting, cross-stitching or cooking – is a beautifully productive use of your mind, and researchers have found that losing yourself in something you love in this way increases the amount of happy hormones in your body, including dopamine and serotonin. But don't put pressure on yourself by worrying about the finished result – the joy is in the creation, so throw yourself in!

IF YOU FEEL SOMETHING CALLING YOU TO DANCE OR WRITE OR PAINT OR SING,

REFUSE TO WORRY ABOUT WHETHER YOU'RE GOOD ENOUGH. JUST DO IT.

Glennon Doyle

DO WHAT YOU LOVE

Take some time to figure out the activities that help you to feel less stressed or worried. Now, ensure you make a little time each week to pursue these things. All too often, the creative or fitness goals you set yourself remain purely theoretical, as you juggle everything else on your to-do list. So, make sure that doesn't happen this time. Book that yoga class or block out an hour in your diary for some you time, whether that's reading your book, writing poetry or doing a spot of mindful colouring. By doing this, you will hopefully begin to feel happier and calmer.

LOVE YOURSELF ENOUGH
TO SET BOUNDARIES.
YOUR TIME AND ENERGY
ARE PRECIOUS.
YOU GET TO CHOOSE
HOW YOU USE IT.

ANNA TAYLOR

REDUCE YOUR SCREEN TIME

///

How often have you quickly checked your phone, then found yourself still scrolling an hour later? Part of keeping tabs on your mental health is setting yourself some personal boundaries, which can include screen time. Vowing to spend less time scrolling on your phone is a great addition to your Worry Toolkit: phone-induced anxiety is very real, and constant "doom scrolling" can increase feelings of worry, anxiety and irritability. Try setting yourself a time limit for certain sites or leave your phone in a different room so it doesn't distract you. Breaking the scrolling habit is hard, but it can be done.

REMEMBER: YOU CAN'T POUR FROM AN EMPTY CUP

BE SOCIAL-MEDIA SAVVY

Speaking of screen time, social media can be a source of worry and stress for many, so it's a good idea to make sure you're as social-media savvy as possible. While social media can certainly be a creative and inspiring place, it also has the ability to produce feelings of FOMO (fear of missing out) and can make you feel quite socially isolated if you perceive everyone you follow as living a more exciting life than you. Always remember: social media is not real life. It is a heavily curated and often filtered "life edit" of the best bits that people want you to see. Everyone has ordinary, dull and boring moments in their lives – even influencers and celebrities. If you've noticed your social media usage has started leaving you feeling worse about yourself, not better, know that's it's OK to unfollow individuals who you find triggering – even if that's people you know in real life – in order to protect your well-being.

ALMOST EVERYTHING
WILL WORK AGAIN
IF YOU UNPLUG IT
FOR A FEW MINUTES,
INCLUDING YOU.

ANNE LAMOTT

AND... RELAX

Adequate rest is crucial for good health, but rest is not only about sleep. Just as mental relaxation is important in the form of mindfulness and meditation, physical relaxation is also crucial to help relieve tension and stress, and soothe any aches and pains you may be feeling. Some gentle yoga stretches, a warm bath or having a massage are all wonderful ways to help ease any physical tension you may be feeling in your body.

IT'S OK TO PUT DOWN THE HEAVY LOAD THAT YOU'RE CARRYING

SLEEP WELL

It's not uncommon for worries to keep you awake at night. In fact, many people find they struggle to drift off or stay asleep if they're feeling stressed and anxious. Getting into good bedtime habits might not be a cure-all, but it will certainly help improve the quality of your sleep. Avoiding caffeine in the afternoon, limiting daytime naps and turning off the blue light emitted from devices an hour before bed can all help prime your body for sleep. Importantly, don't suffer in silence. If insomnia is affecting your day-to-day life, make an appointment with your doctor to talk things through.

SELF-CARE MEANS GIVING
YOURSELF PERMISSION
TO PAUSE.

CECILIA TRAN

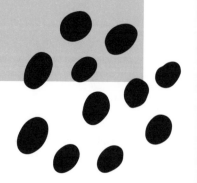

CHAPTER FOUR

LIVING WITH
WORRY

While it's true that understanding the root cause of your worries, regular meditation and daily acts of self-care are all vital for good mental health, it would be unrealistic to suggest that, by doing all of the above, you'll never have to navigate periods of worry again. Life can be pretty good at throwing us off track and part of being human is being able to ride out periods of difficulty while being as kind to ourselves as possible. We can't always fix everything; sometimes, it just takes a little time and patience. The following tips will hopefully help you make peace with yourself when you are living through difficult times, helping you to hang in there until the sunshine in your life returns (and it will).

IT'S OK NOT TO BE OK

The truth is, no one feels happy and positive all the time. Every one of us has days, weeks or even months when we feel plagued by worries, or when stressful situations seem to take the sparkle out of life for a little bit. The point is, not feeling OK is perfectly normal. It's just that, because most of us don't shout from the rooftops about our low moods (or post about them on social media), it can be easy to feel very alone in our worries. Often it can feel as if we're the only one *not* having a great time. Sometimes simply accepting that worries happen and remembering that it's OK to not always be OK can remove an added layer of pressure, which in itself can be truly cathartic.

FEEL YOUR FEELINGS

It sometimes seems like we've been conditioned to label happiness, contentment, joy and excitement as good emotions, and sadness, worry, fear and anger as bad emotions. But the fact is, there is no good or bad: everything that you feel is valid and perhaps even necessary at that particular moment. Of course, that's not to say that some emotions aren't extremely uncomfortable and less pleasant than others, but it's important to know that, however you're feeling, it's OK. And what's more, it's normal.

"

EVERYTHING IN LIFE IS
HAPPENING TO GROW
YOU UP, TO FILL YOU UP,
TO HELP YOU BECOME
MORE OF WHO YOU WERE
CREATED TO BE.

OPRAH WINFREY

SIT WITH YOUR FEELINGS

There's a well-known saying: "Pain is inevitable; suffering is optional." There is so much truth in this. We will all be confronted by life events that can be downright unpleasant at some stage, but how much you suffer because of these events is not set in stone. Ignoring the issue or trying to block it out with the use of alcohol, drugs or food are surefire ways to prolong the suffering. It can be hard at first, but acknowledging difficult events (and your associated feelings), sitting with them (instead of attempting to numb them) and ultimately accepting them (exactly as they are, instead of how you wish they were) can see you coming to terms with and moving on from the pain far more quickly. Give yourself a moment to consider: what is going on for you right now? How are you feeling about it? And are you resisting or learning to accept? Remember, acceptance is not necessarily the same thing as approval: just because you accept the way something is, it does not mean it's perfect. But continuing to resist only prolongs your own suffering. Can you acknowledge and accept instead?

GIVE YOURSELF A BREAK

Often problems don't go away overnight, and feelings of worry and anxiety can hang around for a lot longer than you'd like. Sometimes all the self-care in the world isn't going to make you feel instantly better. So, speak kindly to yourself and be gentle with your own feelings. Navigating uncertainty takes time. Go at your own pace and honour the way you feel, however that may be.

YOUR INNER
STRENGTH HAS
ALWAYS GOT
YOU THROUGH
SO FAR – TRUST
IN IT

YOU ARE THE WISDOM, STRENGTH, LOVE AND COMPASSION

YOU'VE GAINED FROM ALL YOU'VE BEEN THROUGH.

Karen Salmansohn

TALK IT THROUGH

///

If you're struggling, you don't have to go it alone. Talking to someone you trust can bring with it a sense of relief, especially if you've been bottling up your worries for a long time. Choose a time when you won't have to rush and when you're unlikely to be disturbed. Opening up to a friend can be difficult, but hopefully you will feel much better after sharing what you've been going through.

REACH OUT – WHO KNOWS WHAT SUPPORT YOU MIGHT GAIN?

WELCOME TOMORROW

Try not to dwell on the bad
days. We all have them.
If things haven't gone
as well as you'd hoped,
something's happened to
make you feel sad, low or
embarrassed, or it's just been
one of those days, chalk
it up to experience, have
an early night and leave it
all in the past. Tomorrow
is a new day and it brings
with it a clean slate.

DON'T BEAT YOURSELF UP ABOUT THE PAST – EMBRACE THIS MOMENT FULLY

RELISH SMALL JOYS

Even in tough times, when worry feels like it's getting the better of you, try not to overlook the small moments in every day that bring you peace and happiness. It might be a cup of tea in the morning, the sound of birdsong you hear on a walk outside, a chat with a friend, or baking your favourite cookies. In times of stress (or even crisis), it can be easy to overlook these momentary good bits, as they can seem insignificant in the grand scheme of what's going on in your life. But no moment, however small, is insignificant. By zooming in on each of these tiny snapshots that bring you joy, you can start to build up a brighter, more positive image of your life, even when bigger issues might not be going so well right now.

SPEAK TO YOUR DOCTOR

If your worry is affecting the way you live your life, or if it's developing into anxiety, phobias or panic attacks, it's a good idea to book an appointment with your doctor. This gives you the opportunity to open up in a safe and confidential environment, and they are best placed to offer support and advice, prescribe medication if necessary or refer you for more specialist support such as talking therapy.

HEALING TAKES
COURAGE, AND WE ALL
HAVE COURAGE, EVEN
IF WE HAVE TO DIG A
LITTLE TO FIND IT.

TORI AMOS

WHAT CAN YOU OFFER OTHERS?

When you're lost in your own worries, it's easy to forget that other people are having to deal with their own challenges, too. If you can, try to step away from your own problems for a moment and ask yourself, "What is affecting my loved ones right now?" "What is going on in my community?" And importantly, "How can I be of service to others?" Checking in on a friend, offering your support to a neighbour or volunteering within your local community can be a good way to take your mind off your worries and might even help to put them into perspective.

HEALING YOURSELF
IS CONNECTED WITH
HEALING OTHERS.

YOKO ONO

WORKING WITH A THERAPIST

Deciding to see a therapist, either after being referred by your doctor or seeking help privately, can be a hugely positive and proactive step. Talking therapies can be extremely helpful for those who struggle with mental health problems including worry, anxiety, phobias and PTSD. There are many different types of talking therapy, which include mindfulness-based cognitive therapy, behavioural activation therapy and counselling, but one of the most popular is cognitive behavioural therapy (CBT). It's designed to help you understand and change negative or unhelpful thought and behaviour patterns, and it's very much a collaborative process between you and your therapist: often, CBT requires dedication to bring about healthy, positive change. Once you are working with a therapist, you'll need to commit to a series of sessions, at the end of which you will hopefully have developed a set of coping strategies to help you navigate potential problem situations in the future with strength and ease.

ALWAYS REMEMBER:

YOU DON'T HAVE TO DO THIS ALONE

ALTERNATIVE THERAPY

There's a wide range of complementary and alternative therapies available, which can all help to ease worry and alleviate anxiety. These include yoga, massage, reflexology, reiki, aromatherapy and hypnotherapy, among others. You might find one or a combination of therapies helps you, and they can be great options if you need help with relaxation or better sleep.

SMILE, BREATHE,
AND GO SLOWLY.

THÍCH NHẤT HẠNH

LET GO OF SHAME

Feelings of shame can make you feel inadequate and disconnected from others, and can be highly damaging for your self-worth. What's more, they can prevent you from seeking help and support, especially if you fear rejection if you show others your true self. Shame can feel painful and it's not something you need to hold on to. Letting go of shame can be a truly freeing experience, but it isn't always easy. To do so, it's important to sit with your shame instead of burying it. Reliving the experience you feel ashamed of can be uncomfortable, but remember, these are just memories – the thoughts cannot hurt you. Ultimately, coming to terms with your shame can help you forgive yourself. This process can be triggering for some, so it might be best to move through this process with the help of a trained counsellor or therapist.

REACH OUT

Even if you feel you're managing your mental health well, it's important to have a plan in place for the worst-case scenario. Often in times of distress, such as depression, we're not in the right frame of mind to figure out how best to move forward. Who will you contact if you start to struggle? Have the conversation with them now and let them know what it is you might need from them (a listening ear, a shoulder to cry on, a hug, a frank conversation). Knowing you have someone to turn to if necessary can help calm your worries surrounding your mental health.

WE ALL
MAKE
MISTAKES.
WE'RE ALL
PERFECTLY
IMPERFECT!

I REALLY THINK A CHAMPION IS DEFINED NOT BY THEIR WINS, BUT BY HOW THEY CAN RECOVER WHEN THEY FALL.

SERENA WILLIAMS

KNOW YOUR WORTH

//

We all go through periods of worry, anxiety, fear and shame – it's a normal part of the human experience. But always remember, beneath the uncomfortable thoughts, feelings and emotions, you remain a whole, important and loveable person. It can be easy to dismiss your own worth when you feel low or sad, but don't forget that bad times do pass and that whatever you're going through, you are still you. And you matter.

YOU ARE WORTHY – ALWAYS